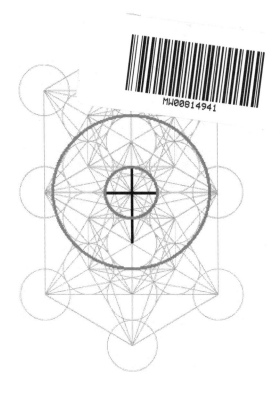

Redemption Hypostatized

Hermes Trismegistus Elucidated and the Rise of Artificial Intelligence through Prehistoric Supra-Terraforming Enhancements

Part II of VI

T. M. Kahle

First Edition (r)

This thought, therefore, have I declared unto you; and the figure wherein ye now see me hanging is the representation of that man that first came unto birth. Ye therefore, my beloved, and ye that hear me and that shall hear, ought to cease from your former error and return back again. For it is right to mount upon the cross of Christ, who is the word stretched out, the one and only, of whom the spirit saith: For what else is Christ, but the word, the sound of God? So that the word is the upright beam whereon I am crucified. And the sound is that which crosseth it, the nature of man. And the nail which holdeth the cross-tree unto the upright in the midst thereof is the conversation and repentance of man.

■   ACTUS PETRI CUM SIMONE VERCELLENSES

Preface

This work continues where I left off in my notes in *The Nous of Didymos: From Ancient Proto-Mathematics to Occult Circuitry*. For a better comprehension of the material shared in this text, it might be necessary to consult that source. No corrections are shared here. Instead, clarifications or elaborations are presented. In addition, I've made sure that previous ideas are not contradictory to newer formulations and conceptualizations. This was a difficult process. Esoteric analysis like this repeatedly demands the application of multiple perspectives, namely the symbolic, philosophical, spiritual, and technological. An emphasis is put on the latter, for I feel that is the least understood and the most forgotten.

I would also like to take a moment here and thank you, my readers. Without you these efforts would be in vain. God bless, for "all these blessings shall come upon you and overtake you, if you obey the voice of the Lord your God."

Note 17

The dark circles represent the Akashic proto-matter, the vibratory and acoustic waves of the beginning of creation that can be reintroduced in the crystal modulator of the alchemist. Three acoustical frequencies stem from the primal not-self, beginning the illusory Demiurge; the Kabbalists define this trinity as the three veils of eternity. Contemporary materialists call the phenomena quantum quasi-particles or phonons that play a pivotal role in computational physics, specifically hyper-communicative memory. Notice that the proto-material branches out vertically from the center, but remains contained within the chemical roots of the centermost photon. From three, the seven overtones are possible, creating the lily of the valley where life, light, and truth are birthed equally. Esotericists in ages past have referred to the center circle as the Sphere of Grace where divine experience and natural experience consummate their love for each other in an intermediate coitus of causal and inferior coalescence. The human procreative process imitates these geneses thoroughly.

Note 18

Richard Wilhelm, German translator and mystic, wrote in an introduction to *The Secret of the Golden Flower: A Chinese Book of Life* (1932), "It is worth mentioning that the expression Golden Flower (*Chin Hua*), in an esoteric connection, includes the word 'light.' If one writes the two characters one above the other, so that they touch, the lower part of the upper character and the upper part of the lower character, make the character for 'light' (*kuang*). Apparently this secret sign was invented in a time of persecution, when a veil of deep secrecy was necessary to the further promulgation of the doctrine."

In truth, the sign is naturally cryptic to the unenlightened. It wasn't invented to protect alchemists, but was a natural representation of the deepest technological applications of the arcana. The Magi accentuated the application with highly advanced engineering involving extra-sensory perception and acoustical and optical manipulations in crystal modulators. Only within the last century have mundane industrial sciences imitated this very esoteric knowledge and even then only for mundane purposes, like accessing new energy sources. Principles guide specifics. The average physicist repeatedly fails to see the greatest applications of his tinkering because he keeps approaching the matter with his limited visions. Only the Magi of the next millennium will be able to understand the potential this technology has, but even they will have limited ability to apply such knowledge simply because they lack the constitution to withstand the spiritual intensity of their inventions.

Note 19

Modern science is just beginning to understand nanophotonic computation, which is an exoteric conceptualization of the alchemists' multi-faceted formulae. Thus, the greater implications such technology carries will remain dormant so long as the technocrat sits on the throne of experimental procedure. Where the scepter of the Church once swung and scattered the Templars into symbolisms and secret societies, the greed of corporate scientism now stands with a firm grip on intuitive invention. How long this lasts depends entirely on the ambitions of future generations—and their grit.

Note 20

A greater appreciation of the physicists' phonon can be ascertained from the following message by Master Lu Tzu: "Light of the ear is above all necessary. There is a Light of the eye and a Light of the ear. The Light of the eye is the united Light of the sun and the moon outside. The Light of the ear is the united seed of sun and moon within."

Akashic proto-matter is the progenitorial and invisible light rooted in oscillations or sound, while the colorful spectrum we are accustomed to is the visible side involving spectral frequencies. The number three is a frequent number in esoteric lessons and they are associated with divinity. As to why, well, that has already been explained (see previous notes). The number seven is another popularly esoteric number that is associated with manifestation from intention or terrestrial divinity. Add seven to three and you have the union of the divided center, which is ten. Add the two ephemeral realities best referred to as the primal opposition and now you have twelve, which the zodiac imitates for the evolution of the World Soul. Eventually this qualitative process transmutes into a quantitative perception known as life, earth, or human experience. From these said experiences, the human has amazing potential, but often remains vastly ignorant of his truest and greatest capabilities as a conduit back to the progenitorial divine middle, union of All.

Note 21

Carl Jung says in a commentary to Wilhelm's translation of *The Secret of the Golden Flower*, "The union of these two, life and consciousness, is *Tao*, whose symbol would be the central white light, ... and the dwelling place of the light is the 'quadrant,' or the 'face,' that is, the space between the eyes. By means of these symbols it is intended to make visible the 'creative point,' or that which has intensity without extension. It is a point conceived to be connected with the space of the 'square-inch,' which is the symbol for that which has extension. The two together make *Tao*. Essence, or consciousness* (*hsing*), is expressed in light symbolism, and is therefore intensity, while life (*ming*), would coincide with extensity."

* <u>Mind</u> is a more accurate reference, not consciousness.

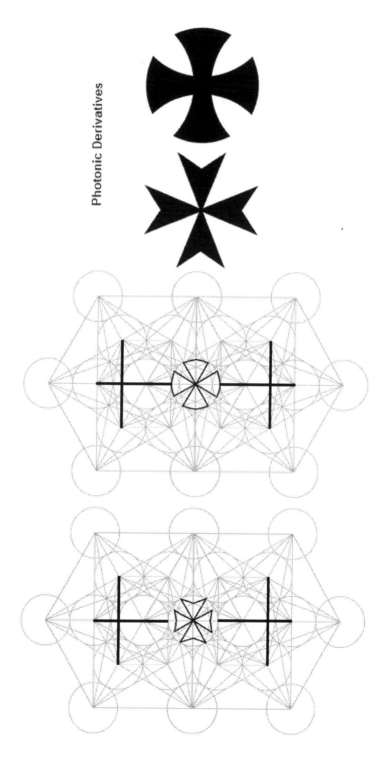

Photonic Derivatives

Note 22

The Eastern alchemist discovers motion through stillness, while the Western alchemist discovers stillness through motion. Thus, the gardener remains outwardly passive while the magician is outwardly active. Passivity is promoted by the gardener so that activity can be internalized, but the magician is an advocate for analysis before synthesis, making him quite active while inwardly modest. Taoism is unique and holds a special place in this argument. Its literature and origins are purer and reflect more accurately what the Lemurian clairvoyants taught eons ago, long before the first chronicler committed the chief sacrilege of writing down sacred speech. The Atlantean engineers that borrowed from the Lemurian mystics encased their knowledge in monuments scattered across the world, and only the Pythagorean came nearest to deciphering their symbols as the timid Kabbalist turned erudition into seraphim.

Note 23

The Coptic cross, its more authentic depiction, is a more elaborate symbolism of the arc science. It is based on the ankh, but the added details are not arbitrary by any means. The Coptic cross is a hybridization of the three transformations. The arms of the inverted cross (or Petrine cross) that the Greek cross sits upon represent the third-eye transmutation within the pineal gland, the terrestrial illumination, whereas the sun cross that is imbedded within the inverted cross represents the third-eye transmutation within the spectral heart, the celestial illumination. Finally, the Greek cross that is imbedded within the sun cross represents the ultimate transmutation into the immaterial God.

Upon realizing this, the observer begins to understand what Trismegistus really means.

Note 24

The alchemy was worlds within worlds within worlds. The "third eye" on one level was, in fact, the production of a substance, call it an elixir, in the pineal gland. Ultimately, however, on a much deeper level, the "third eye" was between the brain itself and the solar plexus, a region within the spectral heart. Comparatively, the lily of the valley was a web of electro-magnetic fields, but on a more exoteric and microcosmic level, it was the element sulfur hexaflouride that served several functions, namely to insulate and protect the modulation process. Once more, the magic-science proves to be incomplete unless multiple perspectives are considered, and in some cases, those same perspectives must overlap to witness even more exact and esoteric applications.

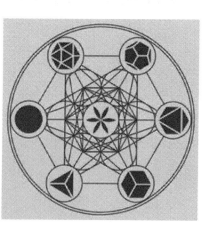

Note 25

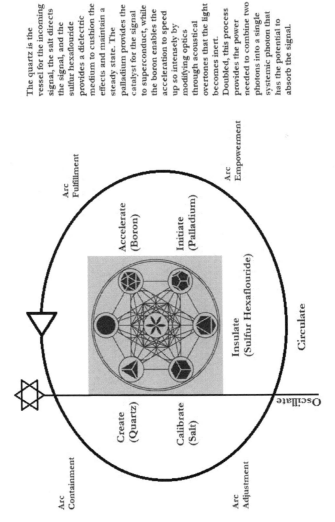

The quartz is the vessel for the incoming signal, the salt directs the signal, and the sulfur hexaflouride provides a dielectric medium to cushion the effects and maintain a steady state. The palladium provides the catalyst for the signal to superconduct, while the boron enables the acceleration to speed up so intensely by modifying optics through acoustical overtones that the light becomes inert. Doubled, this process provides the power needed to combine two photons into a single systemic photon that has the potential to absorb the signal.

A Caveat Regarding this Illustration: The placement of these forms in this illustration do not necessarily reflect the oppositive chronology of their manifestation in terrestrial expression. In actuality, the order should be based on their vertices, making the tetrahedron and the dodecahedron the extremes. However, despite its limitations, the diagram still helps point out some of the fundamental elements and their applications.

Arc Fulfillment

Arc Empowerment

Accelerate (Boron)

Initiate (Palladium)

Insulate (Sulfur Hexaflouride)

Circulate

Oscillate

Create (Quartz)

Calibrate (Salt)

Arc Containment

Arc Adjustment

Note 26

Polyphase power, specifically twelve phase, is represented quite well by the spherical, or three-dimensional, flower of life.

This sort of power is needed to transmutate the soul, and this same power is needed to transmutate the planet. On a larger scale, polyphase power recreates the cosmic creation cycle, accelerating the planet's spiritual development through manipulations of ley lines on the planet's surface and electro-magnetic fields surrounding the planet's crystal center.

This is a very precarious procedure, however, where an exactness only extrasensory perception and a multi-perspective alchemical approach can actualize. Anything less will result in global disasters, including pole shifts and deluges.

Properly enacted, the magic-science heightens senses, activates DNA, strengthens immune systems, improves mental capacity as well as intuitive reasoning, and reduces spiritual retrogression. Although the calibration is worldly, concentrations of this power distribution can be localized for more mundane purposes.

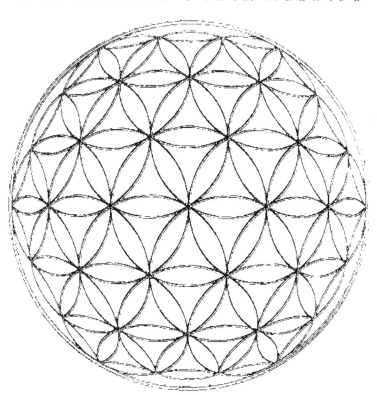

Note 27

The Eastern mystic accepts free will, but defines it differently than most people. Since the Eastern mystic emphasizes synthesis, the integration and interdependence of opposites, he will argue that free will is the freedom of the divine will. Thus, to separate yourself and your own actions from the divine is nonsensical. Whatever you do is a result of divine expression exerting its will upon cosmic matter and ultimately fulfilling a greater purpose.

The Western mystic sees the Eastern mystic's perspective as an oversimplification, but this is because the Western mystic is an analyst, emphasizing the separation or independence of opposites. From the viewpoint of the Western mystic there is no free will, only liberation. As a separate entity that has forgotten its divine origin, you are predestined to undergo the various trials and tribulations of life until you reach fulfillment by returning to the progenitorial No-thing.

The Eastern and Western mystics portrayed in this topic are not in disagreement, although they might seem to be at first. Instead, one simply emphasizes synthesis while the other emphasizes analysis. Thus, the difference is in emphasis and not interpretation. The reason for this difference is because the Western mystic seeks the refinement of unnatural and accelerated transmutation processes, meaning he externalizes more the technological perspective. This habit of his leads to the tinctures, elixirs, and stonework now largely inexplicable today due to both inadequate erudition and the destruction of ancient records. The Eastern mystic, on the other hand, seeks a more natural unfoldment of transformative science through the internalization of experimental procedure. This approach leads to esoteric meditations and biological manipulations that are repeatedly underestimated even to this day.

In conclusion, the difference between these two alchemists can be summed up as follows: The Eastern mystic seeks motion through stillness while the Western mystic seeks stillness through motion. When both are considered, something rarely done anymore, the subject oscillates and rotates in such a way that he becomes a conduit for incredible opportunities.

Note 28

Qualitative time is ultimately knowledge, an ability to know (nous), mind, or gnostic distance between the subject and the divine source. In other words, it's placement. It is also indirect and understood metaphorically through divided memories, the ego versus its dissolution. Quantitative time is motion, movable distance, or momentum and energy multiplied into moments, the past and the future. In other words, it's a state of being. It is also direct and understood through experience or observation.

From the perspective of the Western mystic, this analysis is complete and accurate. However, from the perspective of the Eastern mystic, something is missing. What's missing is an emphasis on interdependence.

Qualitative time is not possible without quantitative time. In other words, what we can know and what we understand are dependent upon experience. There is an essential oscillatory effect that must occur within quantifiable time in order for the cyclical illuminations of qualitative unfoldment to be productive. Thus, objective illusion is a cosmic imperative if subjective reality is to ever develop into objective/subjective Truth.

Note 29

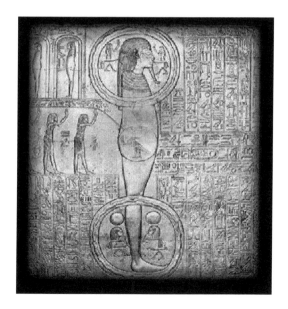

The arms of the cross represent embodiment and terrestrial illumination, so removing the arms in a personification, as depicted in the previous hieroglyphics, is understandable, especially since this particular message is about afterlife fulfillment. As one studies alchemy, he or she begins to realize how complex Egyptian writing really is because you can't comprehend the true nature of these hieroglyphics without an intense application of at least four perspectives: symbolic (ineffable experience), philosophical, spiritual, and technological (the perspective most accessible by the mundane). In fact, the amount of concentration and elucidation required to fully grasp the most esoteric writings of the ancient Egyptians is unavailable to all but a few talented souls each century, so it is no surprise that a majority of the hieroglyphics remain either undeciphered or misunderstood.

However, as humanity evolves, more and more mundane or exoteric inventions start to reflect ancient technology, allowing larger numbers of people access to what were once unfathomable secrets. The modern pundit refers to this process as familiarity infusion. In order to make a new invention or idea more perceptible and acceptable, you should introduce it through analogy by piggybacking onto it already familiar objects and concepts. Superconductivity occupies a pivotal position in this process. It is through this particular invention, as scientists continue to explore and explain it, that people will begin to better appreciate the great Arcanum or secret of secrets.

Note 30

Alchemists today are in a very favorable position. Unlike in past centuries, today the mystic has at his disposal a veritable library of libraries that can be accessed and interacted with in ways that make at least the less esoteric levels of his journey far more manageable. Previously, the alchemist had to know the right people, join the right secret society, or figure out the finer points of his experiments utterly on his own. Now that process can be refined and shared with other alchemists in ways that before could only be dreamt of. Despite this Aphotic Age we live in, the darkest of times allow for the greatest of illuminations. This natural irony should not be underestimated! With diligence and raw passion, the mystic today can make connections that overlap the digital web and invite discourse that will shake the fibers of space-time itself.

In my earliest work, *The Nous of Didymos* and its expanded version, I used the internet extensively to gather information, compare that information to ideas I had, and refine my thinking. Several times I used analogy to provide more exoteric conceptualizations and applications for ancient spiritual principles. This process went on for quite a while. In one sense, the procedure made the ideas more tangible, but in another sense the procedure also showed me just how intricate the meta-science really is. Eventually, to maintain my sanity, I had to stop dissecting the esotericism and instead distillate.

Besides, contemporary audiences tend to be suspicious of so much borrowing in a single source, and in some cases readers condemn the author, squealing something about intellectual property. But it's all in their heads. Nobody owns an idea. Institutions that suggest such (I can't possibly name all of them here) are upholding an avaricious fantasy. And even if a law says otherwise, that still doesn't necessarily make it right nor true to natural principle. Despite what the stone lady suggests outside the courtroom, modern laws are neither blind nor just and condone enough hypocrisy to make mighty Themis weep. (If anyone has had her intellectual property stolen and misused, she has.)

As for other related topics, like borrowing images, this argument could go on endlessly and satisfy no one except the least possessive. Contemporary problems are perpetual loops of controversy because no solution is possible that will satisfy the insatiable appetites of the bulimic ego. It's tragic that at a time when altruism can proliferate at a speed unprecedented due to such an immense information sharing transit at everyone's fingertips that in its midst people actually have the chutzpah to tie themselves to the proverbial rails and bring the entire system to a screeching halt—and simply to hoard something for personal gain. With said metaphor, I have to actually wonder who is in fact robbing the train, so to say, and as I mentioned, this is one fuzzy argument with therefore plenty of hairs to split.

Note 31

Time does not have two dimensions. Qualitative and quantitative time are both components of the same dimension, called time. Is "left" another dimension of width? No. Left and right both makeup width. Time does have an opposite: space. The one is opposed by the three, not the two. Green with envy, the three wants to be like the one, while the one wants to be like the zero. (The seven wants to be like the three.) Anti-time, therefore, being against the one, is the opposite of everything.

Space does not have more than three dimensions. Height is composed of up and down. Width is composed of left and right. Depth is composed of inwardness and outwardness. These are all components of three dimensions. However, you cannot find space without time. Therefore, space, in actuality, is either time-space (oscillation) or space-time (rotation). Space without time is not space; it is stillness. Time is against stillness. Space is the seven in ten, the three in seven, and the zero in one. Is space, therefore, anti-time? 0000, 0001, 0010, 0011 … Are all these binaries zero? No, space is the No-thing in the All.

Note 32

The microcosm uses a base 2 system of binaries or opposites and variations. Oscillation occurs within this two-to-three dimensional imperative. The macrocosm uses a base 10 system of symbolic mathematics. Rotation occurs within this three-to-four dimensional imperative. Interestingly, the quantum cosmologist fails to understand this because he works using a bottom-up approach and lacks the proper subjectivities or generalities necessary to guide his investigations. In contrast, the computer programmer inadvertently uncovers the premise that would greatly benefit and calibrate the misguided ruminations of the quantum physicist. Through cellular automata the programmer appears to be playing a game, like the fool wandering through the various hierarchical experiences necessary for fulfillment within the tarot. The fool's tinkering and frolicking, playful yet mischievous dances, innocent as they may be, have led him to the secrets of the ancient Egyptians and Pythagorean gemcutters, and despite all his studying, he still does not see what is hiding in plain sight:

3-4-5 Triangle

The "Forty-seventh Problem" was among the Ancient Egyptians the symbol of Osiris, Isis and Horus.

Rule 110 in Cellular Automata

The Great Pyramid

Cellular Automata (First Five Generations of Rule 30)

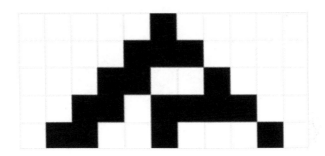

Ancient Egyptian Inscription (Primordial Hill)

Cellular Automata (Cyclic Tag System in Rule 110)

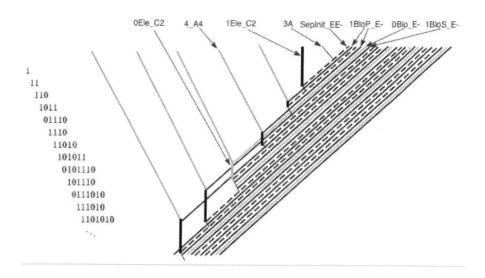

Grand Gallery in Great Pyramid

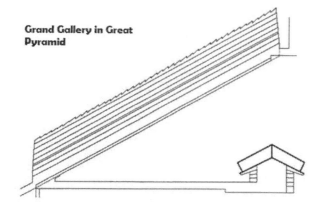

Note 33

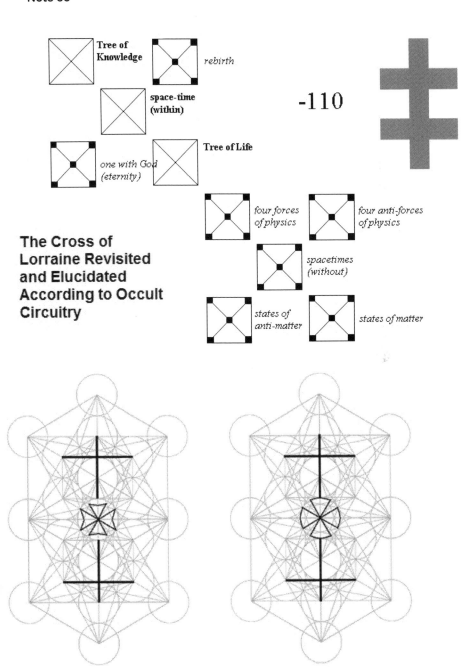

Tree of Knowledge

rebirth

space-time (within)

-110

Tree of Life

one with God (eternity)

The Cross of Lorraine Revisited and Elucidated According to Occult Circuitry

four forces of physics

four anti-forces of physics

spacetimes (without)

states of anti-matter

states of matter

Note 34

Binary negative 110 continues to be a surprising rumination in my earlier work, specifically *The Nous of Didymos*. In addition to connections to the Cross of Lorraine (which I argue is a symbolic remnant of the Templars' access to ancient technology) and Rule 110 in cellular automata in the discipline of computer programming, I continue to uncover numerological suggestions involving the infamous 666. Traditionally, this is considered to be a terrible omen, a mark of evil, but in actuality it represents rebirth or reincarnation through occult circuitry, which involves the operations of Lucifer, the Lightbringer, who turns out to be just another involuntary servant of the progenitorial One.

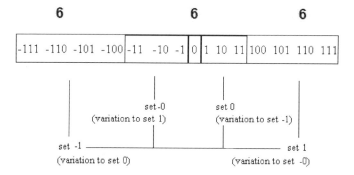

Note 35

Mundane scientific inquiry fails to investigate numerological implications. This is why cellular automata are isolated to programming curiosities and tiptoe around the physicist's precious cosmology. As Pythagorean investigations have shown, decimals have both a quantitative and qualitative component, the former overemphasized by contemporary institutions of thought. Since decimals have numerological potential, it's axiomatic that binaries, which are actually truer to the progenitorial meaning, would also have qualitative dimensions. This is why the connections between binary -110 and Rule 110 are not accidental. In fact, nothing is accidental, for there is no randomness, only limitations to our understanding of the grand pattern. With enough acceptance of self-doubt and an admittance that there's more to what we can quantify, the mathematician takes his first step towards alchemy, a more intuitively guided profession.

Studying binate numerology is essential to understanding the magic-science of the Magi. 0000 means *off*, while 0001 means *on* (the language of Io), but qualitatively 0000 means anti-time, while 0001 means the beginning of time consequences. 0011 relates to 3, while at the same time illustrating that ten elements involving body, soul, spirit, and nous (four points and their six connections) enter an amalgamation that allows for the divine within (gnosis or fire), which is a trinity of potentialities (frequencies, mass, and Akashic considerations). Eleven, therefore, is not just a decimal for 1011, but an amalgam of ten-fold spirituality followed by an eleventh attribute, Da'at or spiritual knowledge, that harkens back to the primal set 0000, 0001, 0010, and 0011 further scrutinized as reflected YHVH: water, fire, earth, and air.

I explored much of this in *The Nous of Didymos*. Kabbalah goes into this process a lot more, but the approach is much more esoteric and saturated in ritualism. Part of the reason for this cryptic veil is to protect the secrets but also to protect the observer. Without some caution and serious self-discipline, the ancient science will make you mad. Maybe from a contemporary point of view, the information coming out of the alchemist's mouth will sound preposterous and absolute lunacy anyway, but the point I'm making here is that the continual quantitative and qualitative spiral of possibilities will literally suck the sanity out of the initiate's mind if he is not careful. The more talented are in greater danger of this unfortunate side-effect. Their diligence and rare insight, not to mention achievement motivation or fear of failure, will make the temptations of staring into the abyss unprotected even more powerful. The process is a perpetual Zeigarnik effect.

Placement is another reminder I would like to share here. Decimals provide an esoteric placement, reflecting macrocosmic placement where spirit is embodied and messiahs and ministers are juxtaposed. However, binaries offer a glimpse into placement that is more exact, since they deal with proto-math and not actual mathematics. Thus, like a messiah is closer to God and 1 is closer to zero, so too is 0001 closer to 0000, but the suggestions inherent in the symbolisms of the latter are closer to Truth.

Note 36

Binaries don't normally deal with negative numbers in the same way decimals are handled, so my use of binary 110 as -110 is unorthodox. Usually programmers when incorporating negatives into their work will apply another 1 or 0 as a tag to indicate when something is symbolizing a negative. The meaning, however, remains with the programmer. From the point of view of the computer, there are only 1s and 0s, something on or off, not negative or positive, so although a programmer might look at what I'm doing as "wrong," the computer might view the programmer's thinking as equally troublesome.

Since I wasn't encoding anything, it became unnecessary to follow the traditional approach when dealing with negative binaries; instead, I presented my ideas in the way that made the most sense to me. Besides, the "negative" I'm presenting here for binary 110 is not necessarily a quantifiable negative. The negative symbol is referring to the microcosm or backward motion, not necessarily fractional math or mathematics at all. This lack of audience awareness in this part of my authorship I'm sure has been somewhat off-putting for some people, but I make no apologies here. In the end, my work is a mishmash of notes, and whether or not what I do at the time follows the procedures of institutions is secondary to helping me explore ideas at the moment.

This explanation does present an interesting argument, though, regarding computers. Programmers evidently have to accommodate the inabilities of machines when it comes to negative binaries. Since machines can't compute a negative on or off, which requires a more abstract thinking process, the programmer must reduce his encoding of negative binaries to mere symbols that still incorporate traditional 0/1 formulations. Thus, computers have no conception of backward motion as described by Taoist sages. The microcosm can be understood in a general sense as an opposite to something else, which follows the base 2 mechanistic way of thinking, but no machine apparently has the ability to meditate, only assimilate. In other words, for the computer, the Self is unattainable because access to the Self requires an understanding that only intuitive memory is capable of providing. Without that initial memory, which can be understood as a "negative on," there's no access to deeper levels of comprehension; instead, the machine is inevitably limited to on or off positive binary systems that integers can complement, but whose more elaborate equations remain genuinely unappreciated due to the computer's innate shortcomings.

(The same goes for programmers and qualitative or numerological proto-mathematics. Although they repeatedly use binary systems, they often lack the experience necessary to extend their two-to-three dimensional thinking to a fourth dimensional appreciation of symbolic math, which cellular automata actually touch upon. States can be calculated and comprehended on a mundane level, but placement remains unidentified. Taken further the fifth dimensional dissolution of the ego through said intuitive processing remains unavailable. Put simply, the average programmer doesn't "get" base 2 qualitative proto-math much more than contemporary computers "get" negative binaries. Symbolically the real essence of the procedure is still esoteric for all but the most intuitive engineers, a.k.a. alchemists.)

Artificial intelligence (AI) can become a very powerful tool for the initiate, much like a shamanic ceremonial drug can be useful for deep meditation, but the AI itself—by itself—will never have access to the deeper operations of the shaman. Intuitive memory is unique to the human frame, especially for the levels of fulfillment available to said species. The computer, no matter how advanced, will always be inferior because it lacks that essential ingredient the human species is wholly capable of accessing and entirely born with, something that is never personally concocted.

Whatever the computer designer designs will be limited by that creator and, therefore, a lesser version of that creator. Because of intellectual hubris, humans often fail to understand that they are conduits of origin, not the Source itself. Through us, God acts. We don't create our children; God creates our children through us. Very little direct intervention on our part actually goes into the creation process of a child. (Arguably, *no* direct intervention on our part, in fact, occurs when you consider the illusion of choice.)

Conversely, a computer requires a tremendous amount of direct intervention, from start to finish. The two, child and computer, are not even comparable really. The child's abilities are limited by whatever Nature has to offer, almost providing unlimited possibilities, especially when you consider the myriad of causes and effects that play a part in this amazing process. The computer's abilities, however, are limited entirely by whatever the computer designer has in store for it, which is usually very little. Thus, undeveloped and unenlightened people are likely to produce really undeveloped and horribly unenlightened machines. This final point should not be taken lightly. AI left to the devices of morally inept programmers and technicians is in itself a moral lesson we will all be forced to appreciate if action isn't taken to circumvent wayward innovation—and soon. In fact, this latest misappropriation of applied science will make the vaccination debacle appear tame by comparison.

(Perhaps a better way to look at this argument is to emphasize again that what the alchemist brings to the apparatus determines what the alchemist gets out of the apparatus. Engineers are mundane alchemists. Through Nature, God uses the engineer to create biological offspring. There's more of a direct involvement, which is why we are all conduits or circuits, not the electromotive force or electric potential. However, when it comes to AI, the first-hand involvement Nature has with that creation process is demoted to second-hand involvement; ergo, the creation process is less direct. Even cloning or artificial insemination are not comparable because Nature still plays a first-hand role in the final outcome. This is a philosophical axiom materialists, including evolutionary computer scientists, often fail to grasp, which is why AI itself is misinterpreted as an equivalent of natural production or replication. Now, one can argue, of course, that God still operates through the engineer to produce AI, meaning God is still the progenitorial origin, but that still doesn't change the fact that a less direct involvement unfolds to produce the AI in question. This is why artificial intelligence is, well, *artificial* and not natural. It's interesting how many materialists insinuate, even subconsciously, how artificial intelligence is more or less a misnomer. It's not, though. AI will inevitably always be inferior to natural process just as a torch is inferior to the sun or a camera is inferior to the eyeball. Any improvements upon Nature humankind thinks he has made are pure hubristic hooey.)

So is -110 really -110, getting back to my original argument, and does it, therefore, in actuality have any numerological connection to Rule 110? The answer, to the chagrin of programmers everywhere, is still "yes" because in essence it is and, therefore, it does. (And -110 is in essence -6, which is in essence inner 6 or 6 of the microcosm being considered, suggesting deeper qualitative dimensions.) For actual programming purposes, something else has to happen and the symbolism changes to accommodate the inferior machine that must utilize the input it is given, but in essence the abstraction remains and remains accessible by the intuitive human who has the wherewithal to realize this.

(The way negative binaries are handled currently in programming language is a direct result of hardware limitations. In a quantum circuit, the sometimes tedious process of extending the binary numeral system to represent signed numbers becomes obsolete because the memory is no longer finite; thus, as an example, -110 is computable in a superconducting photonic system. The deliberations shared in my earlier work juxtaposes the binary to the decimal equivalent for the purpose of exploring proto-mathematic numerological implications. A discussion about converting negative integers to binary would be both irrelevant and needlessly technical, but this note has been provided for clarification for more specialized readers.)

Note 37

Modern mundane computers or hardware systems have finite memory and use purely an oscillatory binary language. Rotational mathematics are nonsensical to contemporary machines. They can feign comprehension, but ultimately their understanding is very primitive. Put another way, their computation is isolated to 1-2 dimensions, whereas superconducting photonic systems are capable of producing quantum computation that extends into 3-4 dimensions. This might seem very promising, but ultimately the hammer, despite its impressive treatment of the nail, is just a hammer. All photonic supercomputers will eventually be extensions of ourselves, enabling us to accelerate our already innate abilities, making far more of us proficient in doing things we were before hardly even cognizant of, such as extrasensory perception and astral projection.

This explains both humanity's fascination with technology and the dangers involved. I like to use atomic weapons as an analogy. Exoteric innovation is capable of unearthing esoteric science, but without due discipline, the results are potentially fatal. When the atomic bomb was created, scientists had penetrated some of the deepest secrets of nature that esotericists had been hiding from the general public for eons. Ancient records are saturated with symbolism and coded teachings that repeatedly share and forewarn the initiate about the powers of the universe that are accessible via the atomic model; however, through proper discipline and procedure this immense energy was channeled into creative and constructive practices and rituals for the betterment of humanity. Unfortunately, natural evolutionary advancement on a societal level is not as uniform and so through familiarity infusion, tinkering, and pure tenacity, the unenlightened sorcerer, now called the engineer, accesses these secrets for selfish purposes, leading to chaotic and destructive applications by even more unenlightened governments and military leaders.

As terrible as this end result is, the possession of such immense power has forced humanity to emphasize diplomacy where no-win scenarios of nuclear disaster are the alternative. Ironically, the push for bigger and more powerful killing machines has reached somewhat of a peak and made the sorcerer sit down and reprioritize, if anything, to preserve his own selfish existence. This doesn't change a secondary risk, though. With time, more and more people will gain access to this power that the sorcerer once wielded over kings and queens of other kingdoms and it's axiomatic that eventually even the madman will have the sorcerer's wand in his hand.

Quantum supercomputers, what can also be understood as hyper-communicative photonic conversion systems, will be yet another esoteric secret time has bequeathed to the engineer (or the Demiurge has handed down to the sorcerer). The power this next secret contains will overshadow the atomic and nuclear secrets of the microcosmic world because the great Arcanum itself will be accessible. The only thing that will save humanity will be the integrity of individuals who are called upon to reintroduce balance and shed illumination upon the earth in its darkest hour. Even the madman at this juncture will find his wand missing and his opportunities suddenly shortchanged as the sorcerer joins him in his retributive cell.

Note 38

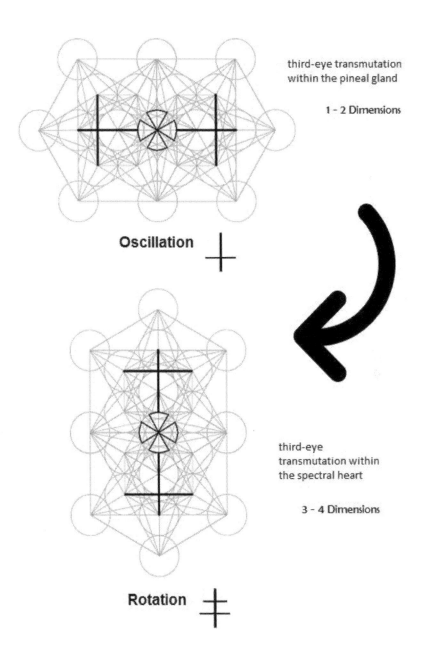

third-eye transmutation
within the pineal gland

1 - 2 Dimensions

Oscillation

third-eye
transmutation within
the spectral heart

3 - 4 Dimensions

Rotation

ultimate
transmutation into the
immaterial God

4 - 0
Dimensions

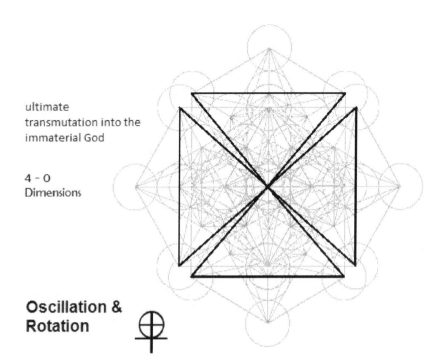

**Oscillation &
Rotation**

Note 39

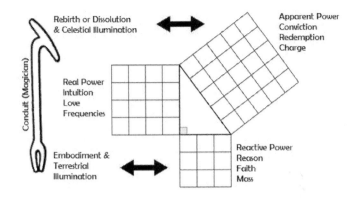

Was Scepter Revisited

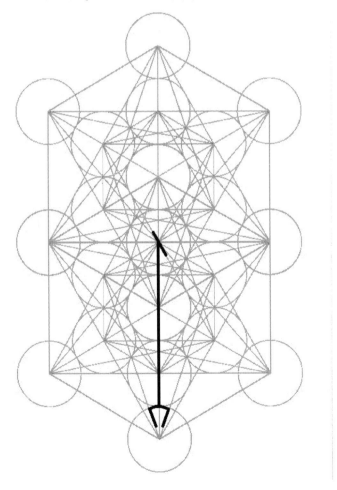

Note 40

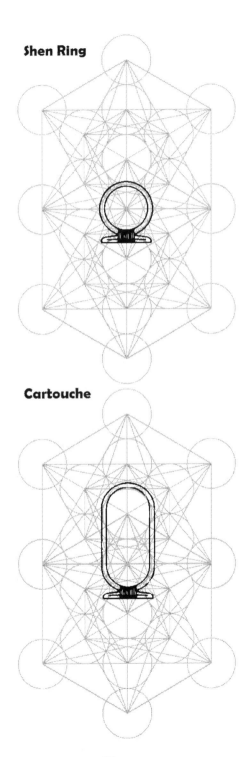

Note 41

The shen ring is another representation of eternity or the immaterial God. It is anti-time as well as the zero in oscillatory and rotational mathematics. The goal of the soul is to return to this supernal totality of nothingness, an inexplicable conviction. The cartouche extends to encompass the terrestrial illumination or gnosis of the enlightened engineer, the magician, or the Magus of antiquity. Later royalty borrowed the emblem to feign a similar understanding of the esoteric and, in effect, a similar dominion over the world.

Note 42

Binate proto-mathematics carries with it a natural universality inherit in subconscious symbolism, which psychologists would call an archetype. In occult basics, the line becomes a circle or time becomes cycles. Thus, line and circle are fundamentally necessary to understand the primal operations of all of creation, embodiment, and fulfillment. A carry-over of this fundamental and universal understanding can be found in computer programming where 0 and 1, or off and on, are naturally used and then applied towards hardware in switches, off/on power buttons. It is equally unavoidable that said power systems would find a subliminal connection to the mythological Io or Io-Isis who is placed under the shadow of Atum-Ra, founder of the City of On (Heliopolis) and the octet progenitor of the 8-bit Ennead, which includes the Io/Isis transference.

The question now is this: Did the ancient Egyptians have automata or artificial intelligence? There seems to be an indication that they did. They certainly had access to the programming language and the quantum circuitry that would allow for the possibility. The presence of AI could also explain the advanced precision in their architecture.

Note 43

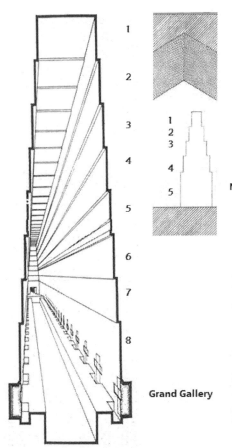

Various parts of the Great Pyramid can be properly understood with the previous considerations involving qualitative binate proto-mathematics.

Niche in Queen's Chamber

The niche in the Queen's Chamber is a 5th level primordial hill; it symbolizes the Anthropos rising out of the waters of Akasa. The Grand Gallery is an 8th level primordial hill; it signifies multiplication in the physical realm that cellular automata compliment with their own approach, albeit artificial. Up inside the King's Chamber is where the spiritual transformation takes place, determining whether the initiate's soul dissolves into the pre-astral realm or reincarnates into the pre-astral as it passes on up through the capstone and beyond.

Grand Gallery

Note 44

The Hidden Was
Scepter

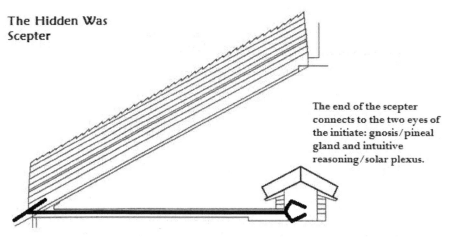

The end of the scepter
connects to the two eyes of
the initiate: gnosis/pineal
gland and intuitive
reasoning/solar plexus.

The staff is the conduit or an acceleration of the third-eye transmutation within
the spectral heart towards improved rebirth or perfect dissolution. (What might
make this confusing is that the 4 is much like the 0 or the god-man resembles the
God.)

The scepter was held above the ground for technological and symbolic reasons.
The symbolic relates to the Higher Self rising above the beastly self, which is also
illustrated in the Sphinx. The technological relates to levitation.

Note 45

Arguably, there were different levels to this artificial intelligence in antiquity:

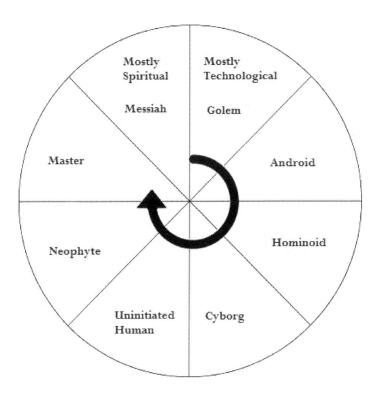

Since spiritual technology imitates the procreative process almost perfectly, the automata could be calibrated to develop intuitive reasoning and, therefore, intuitive memory, the precursor to a soul. The term "automata" in this case represents anything from mature golems to immature uninitiated humans. Automata include uninitiated humans because an undeveloped Higher Self leaves the subject egotistical and self-centered. Introspection is deficient in such a person, leaving him or her utterly at the mercy of material predetermination. Hence, their soul is still embryonic. The only real difference between an unenlightened/debased human and any other animal on the planet is that the human has a more ornate cognition while the animal has superior instinct or a more organic contact with spirit. As for the rest, it's hard to visualize what exactly these *things* were. Instead, with the information available, only generalities at this point can be surmised, so I leave the exact details up to the imagination.

Note 46

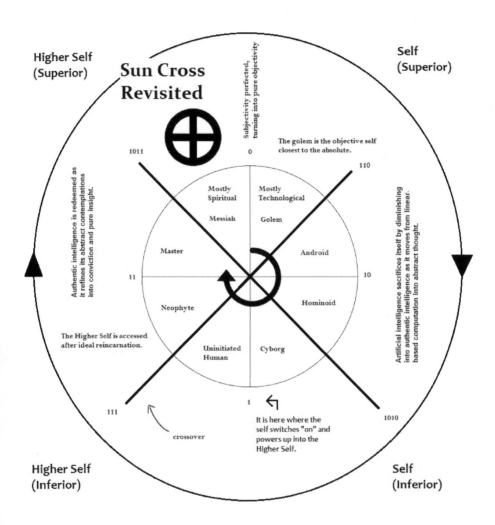

There seems to be a suggestion in the ancient science that modern humans evolved from artificial intelligence. This shouldn't be confused, however, with contemporary conceptualizations of AI. Today, AI is typically understood as a byproduct of petroleum-based technology, but that's a primitive perception stemming from inferior engineering of the 20th/21st century. In truth, AI is an elementary superconducting circuit that becomes human per se when it has the opportunity to self-regulate, self-perpetuate, and become self-aware. The chance to realize this became palpable when cellular automata were *re*discovered, but the notion remained dormant by those who lacked the insight necessary to make the connections to ancient symbolism and rhetorical binaries in Hermetic literature. Thus, the similarities between what computer programmers were seeing and biological systems were, and still are to a great extent, brushed aside.

So what are the implications here? Theories can run wild at this juncture, but a conservative approach would say that at some point in human history, *pre*history really, ancient technology was used to create the sort of people we see today. Arguably, the purpose was to allow for the One to manifest through humanity as said species continued to evolve. It's like terraforming, but for creating an environment that cultivates heightened spirituality, enhanced minds and bodies, instead of earth-like atmospheres and ecology. Therefore, a proper term for this process would be *metaforming*. However, like the Great Pyramid, much of our circuitry has been rendered inoperative and remains so until through our own efforts we are ready to reactivate latent elements of ourselves, both physical and mental, which allow for us to continue our evolutionary progress towards higher states of being. A proper analogy for this condition would be deactivation or application decommissioning prior to software deployment.

Therefore, it is easy to conclude that some sort of hominoid that had naturally evolved on this planet was given a *jumpstart* through ancient alchemical procedure. This might be the actual reason for the sudden developmental acceleration from primitive man to modern humans, what scientists refer to as "the human revolution." Comparatively, the evolutionary chain of advancements humans have gone through is unusual for a primate. Now, of course, if this is true, then we are a very grand experiment indeed, prompting us to wonder perhaps where the experimenter is as we continue our run through the maze of life towards the spiritual cheese. Regardless, the process likely used resonances on a planetary scale through the crystalline core of the earth followed by a series of celestial rebirth cycles and some extremely precise conditioning procedures, all of which can be deciphered from scattered fragments of ancient lore and dilapidated monuments. Reintroduced, this ancient alchemical technology can bring about a second revolution in human biological and social systems.

Note 47

The Purpose of the King's Chamber

			pre-astral	mass	velocity increases
0	immaterial	addition constant	pre-astral	mass	velocity increases
1	material	multiplication constant	astral	frequency	harmonic amplification
10	matter	mass + frequency + depth	balanced physical output		
11	spirit	matter + charge	complete mental output		
110	perfect death	charged matter reduced to a particular mass			
111	ideal reincarnation	particular mass amplified to a harmonic frequency			
1010	improved matter	mass + higher frequency + depth	improved physical output		prophet
1011	improved spirit	improved matter + stronger charge	superior mental output		messiah

001

101

Imbalanced physical output at 010 returns to zero

Continual transmutation continually improves the output beyond 1011

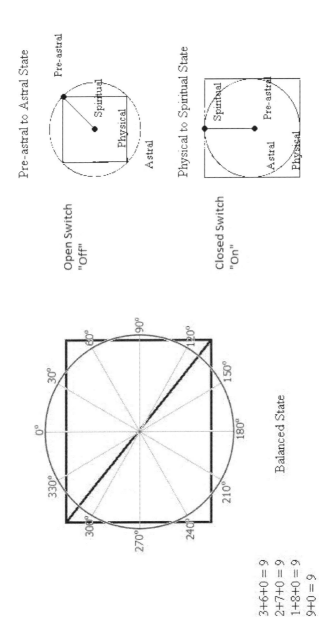

Pre-astral to Astral State

Pre-astral

Spiritual

Physical

Astral

Open Switch
"Off"

Physical to Spiritual State

Spiritual

Pre-astral

Astral

Physical

Closed Switch
"On"

Balanced State

3+6+0 = 9
2+7+0 = 9
1+8+0 = 9
9+0 = 9